First published by Botsotso in 2023
59 Natal St
Bellevue East
Johannesburg 2198
botsotso@artslink.co.za
www.botsotso.org.za

ISBN: 978-1-990922-67-1

In the text © Anton Krueger 2023

Acknowledgements

Writing included in this collection has previously appeared in *New Coin, Itch, Aerodrome, Ons Klyntij, Aerial, New Contrast, Kotaz* and *Bombay Gin*. The "revolutionary diaries" were published in *Experimental Writing: Africa vs Latin America, Vol. 1*, edited by Ricardo Félix and Tendai Mwanaka (2017). "A Bad Spell," formed part of the South African edition of *Imagined Theatres* (2017), edited by Megan Lewis. "Moving House" was published in *Coming Home* (2019) edited by Harry Owen and "the programmable bride" appeared in a volume edited by Tendai Mwanaka, *Writing Robotics: Africa Vs Asia Vol 2* (2020).

Many thanks to Inma Garcia-Carrasco for graciously allowing use of her artwork for the cover. Inma is a figurative artist based in the South of Spain, however, a brush with Japanese Calligraphy, born from a deep-seated passion for Japanese culture, adds a unique dimension to her portfolio. With several successful exhibitions in London and a global reach, her work not only reflects the vibrant Spanish landscapes but also weaves in the elegance of Japanese tradition, creating a captivating fusion that resonates across cultures and continents. To see more of her work, visit: www.inmagc.co.uk.

Cover image: Inma Garcia-Carrasco
Ensos for section headings: Anton Krueger
Layout and design: James de Villiers

to Aman Bloom
friend & collaborator

CONTENTS

Close to Home

My Sister Sonia 1
The Telegraph Inspector 3
Louise & her Lux Bug 5
Unwinder 6
Uncle Noodle 7
Eulogy for Willem Huyzers 9
When 11

Moving House

Naropa Poem 15
The Wooden Veranda 19
Heimwee 22
One Settler, One Pothole 23
Afraid of Birds 25
Moving House 26

After Watching

Between One & Two Metres 28
Poor Seraphine 31
Nichts Neueus 33
Herder 34

Kinds of Wild

Channelled 37
Longing for a Rut 38
Kinds of Wild 39
Wilderness 41

Prosaically
10 Characters 45
Imaginary Theatres: A Bad Spell 48

smallcaps
the programmable bride 53
ten thousand hands 57
so i had this really 58
clint's koan 59
at the funeral 60

notes
garbage 63
notifications 64
in two hours, i will have been awake for twenty-four 65
questionnaire 67
everybody is a bridge 68

fragments
revolutionary diaries (tryp on anxious conflicts) 71
you see the devil everywhere 73
hope 74
on turning 40 75
the writer 76

My Sister Sonia

When we were kids, my older sister Sonia used to sing.
All the time. Constantly.
In the car. Driving off on holidays, down to the library,
or just out for bread and milk.

Abba, mostly. Or the children's gospel pop we'd learnt at
church. Just singing away. Quite loudly. Often out of key.

What a show-off. I'd ask my mom to tell her to stop.
She can't even sing. Sounds stupid. Just shut up already.

Sonia would laugh, or tease me, or sulk ...
But then one day – she stopped singing.

And when we drove off on family holidays,
Sonia wouldn't sing along anymore.

Even when my dad played the Greatest Hits,
she would just sit silently staring
at the mute world going by.

Remembering this, I felt bad.
Tell Louise, I've got to fix this.

My sister Sonia picks up the phone in PE 30 years later.
She's surprised to hear from me. I say, I've been thinking ...

Yes?
I need to tell you –
What?
I know it might seem silly,
but I need to say I'm sorry ...

The line goes quiet.
There's a pause.

And then she says –
This isn't about the singing again?
Every few years you apologise.
Forget it, I love you.
And anyway, I never stopped.

And she hums a few bars from Dancing Queen,
before clicking off the call.

The Telegraph Inspector

My great-great-great-grandfather
was a Telegraph Inspector ...
This would have been Germany, 1800's.
Wearing a big old square white beard,
he appears all serious for his portrait.

I mean, he's a Telegraph Inspector, right?
You'd need to have your beard pretty square and trim
to walk in, going: "I'm here to inspect your apparatus."

Telegraph operators weren't permitted
great big old square white beards, oh no.
They couldn't be trusted.
A follicle might fall between the clapper
and the clapped upon.

Operators would have to be clean, fresh shaven.
Could sport a dapper moustache only
if you were well behaved, a favourite.

Maybe my great-great-great would test them on their
Morse, going – "Wilhelm? What is
dot dot dot / dash dash dash / dot dot"?
And Wil would scramble: "Uh ... S ... O ... uh ..."
And – (because it was a trick question),

My great ³ˣ ᵍʳᵃⁿᵈᶠᵃᵗʰᵉʳ would go: "Too slow."
And then you were out!

You were out there on the avantgarde
of information technology.
You were sending signals from over the earth,
under the oceans even.
Confirming your being
by the poetry of the dots and the dashes.

You needed a big old square beard from within which
to purse your lips at those fingertips tapping:
   —— .—.. —.. / .—— .... .. — . /
   —... . .— —. —.. / .. ... / .... . .—. .

Louise & her Lux Bug

Louise lionises that Beetle –
big old copper gold Volkswagen
that rattles and roars every dawn.

She primes it and polishes it,
paints out every scratch,
she wraps it up in nylon every night.

I've tried to lead her to reason,
tell her it's getting old now,
time to get it sold now

It's battery's bound to bomb
three times a winter season.
but no, Louise loves that Lux Bug.

Her stubbornness irritates,
her obsessiveness infuriates ...

And yet, one day when my gears grate,
when my seats are torn and my engine's worn,
I hope she won't be trading me in either.

Unwinder

She's unaware of how she twists the landline up
when cradling phone to shoulder.
She'll be turning round and chattering,
while fussing with the desk's utensils,
knotting it and tangling cable into twisted mess.

But when she's not looking, he's learnt,
to hold it up at one end, let the wire spin out,
let gravity relax the cable, ease it open,
stretching out its angry turns.

Similarly, the garden hose.
From his days as a roadie, he knows
you need to loop a quarter twist
to keep the cable supple
to retain its default spring.

Sometimes, he secretly untightens
the lids of jars he knows she needs.

Uncle Noodle

"Ah," he said, when I saw him the last time,
"Now you find out who really cares ..."

Uncle Noodle had always been my favourite.
In a world where adults were there
to state, to judge, declare –
he was indecisive, unsure, insecure,
sometimes wretched, often defeated.

His heart had chasmed
in the wake of his wife's leaving;
when she'd divided him from dignity,
collapsed his happiness machinery.

I remembered him howling in our garden, as
a posse of therapists "managed" him to the ground;
silencing his grief with a needleful of numbness,
stopping his fight for the right to end his life.

We laughed about the others in the ward:
one obsessively folding / unfolding / refolding a paper,
another sycophantically praising the awful food.
We joked about the blunt strokes of the Casiotone
the old dame played next door.

When they moved him to his final room, they'd
removed boxes and boxes crammed with slides
– ten thousand, twenty – a lifetime's worth
of proof when he'd been alive.

Vast accumulation of his lonesome wanderings,
were rubbished as unstorable.
Now his kidneys hadn't been on the job,
his stubby fingers fattened to yellow,
the waste inside, unshorable.

Uncle Noodle had dragged himself
through so many dreadful days,
used up all his cliches,
had no more choices left.

I stroked his head, said, "It's okay,"
soothed eyes bewildered by fear.

What else to say? How ease his pain?
"I'm sorry about your slides," I said.

Eulogy for Willem Huyzers

Hurt child lashing out
tried to seduce my girlfriend,
abandoned me in Hatfield;
saw himself as Caulfield,
everybody else as phoney.

In Durban after drinking,
forgot his key, so, casually
smashed a window in, and
Jan raced him to Emergency
to stitch the blood back in.

Looking out at on that dark sea,
cradling his injured wrist,
Willem said he was ship
without anchor ...
                    ... adrift ... adrift ... adrift ...

Driving back to Pretoria,
Jan was taunting Laura.
It was getting stuck, so –
"Hou nou op met hierdie kak!"
Willem screamed the subject closed.
Intense snot spooling down
the tip of his Roman nose.

New Year's Eve in Rose Street,
dived in dirty pool with black jeans,
hit his head on concrete,
blood running down his face.

It was the new millennium,
Willem shivering in the lounge,
seemed sad but determined, said:
"You're the only one I've loved."

The last time I saw him,
I'd just flown in from Shanghai.
He was cancerous on a sofa
in his mother's old age home.
Happy to see me – but he stank.
Had to crack a window open not to gag.

Showed him pictures from China;
we sat and watched the ducks fly.
His mother gave us cup-cakes
she'd bought for Mandela Day.

Shot a video of his shadow on my phone.
Never saw him alive again.

When

When my grandmother was dying,
we stood around her bed, singing hymns.
Her gaunt spectral body splayed out, thin;
in her eyes, something wild,
already seeing Glory ...

When Alex died, he was asleep.
Had taken pills and slipped beneath
the waters of a London park.
A peaceful place to go,
he'd told her, though
his actions shattered family,
shrapnelled bitterness through friends ...

When Hunter S. Thompson died,
Evan was angry: couldn't Dubya
have killed himself instead?

When Chris Hani died, I was on a not-quite date
with the niece of his assassin.
She said: "Next time you won't be sick ..."

When Saddam Hussein died,
I was near Caracas in a seaside town –
wood panelling all the walls of the room.
Infatuated by a stranger,
walked the shoreline daily
to write in a freezing internet café ...

When Willem died,
his family recused themselves,
because he had refused their God, and
Jan was furious all the way to Pretoria ...

When Margaret died,
her patients came from all around,
remembering her curiosity, her innocence.
She told me once she had no clients,
only friends ...

Brendon died a year or so ago, and
still sometimes I dream of him.
Last night saw him adancing,
laughing in a high-rise apartment;
no railings on the sides, holes in the floor.
Frightened, I tried to fix things with his landlord,
who remained evasive, kept her clipboard close,
continued checking the canals ...

When Gruva died, Lama Yeshe said he'd caught her,
and Dave floated her ashes down the Marico ...

When Sula died,
we buried her in the garden,
and blamed each other ...

When my mother was a little girl,
she saw a horse step on a hatchling,
and she laughed.

Naropa Poem

(Written for the Summer Writing Programme at the Kerouac School of Disembodied Poetics at Naropa University in Boulder, Colorado, 2016. The borrowed lines of dada are from Kurt Schwitter's Ur Sonata.)

>Naropapoem
>Naropapapapap poem
>Naropapapapapapapap poem
>"Fumms bo wo ta za goo pogiff – "

... is what I thought of saying when Tara mentioned liking Dada just before handing me the mic on Monday ...

But I lost my nerve mid-reach, costing hours of mental fuss on how things could have been if I'd only managed spontaneously to splash out, going –

>*fumms po wo ta zo goo pogiff ...*

Would you have liked me more or less? Been less or more impressed ... or couldn't care less? Would the barometer of average happiness in the room have been raised, or would it have added confusion for those not into the Ur Sonata?

Fums bo wo – I'm in America for a week, with its broad sidewalks, clean creek, sweeping sky ... coffee bags open smooth, the nuts rezip, appliances come with plugs attached, everything is easy ... feels like I'm in a movie or on a sitcom set coz everyone around me is talkin' American:

> *"How ya doin'?"*
> *"Got everything ya need?"*

In my first 48 hours I speak to ten people ... nobody asks where I'm from, though the woman at Safeway does say, a little suspiciously:

> *"You're not from America, are you?"*

And I have to ... hesitate, and say, well ... no, not actually ... though it feels America has colonized me and my subconscious stream ... the music and the movies washing into my dreams ...

Makes me feel uneasy ... a bit like maybe like maybe like maybe I'm an inadequate American, you know, an amputee, somebody who should have known better than to have been born in Africa ...

> *"Must be nice, I've never left the state."*

In the library at Naropa, I meet Dennis Brutus and Madiba,
but not Chris Barnard, not Breytenbach, nor the guy who
invented the Kreepy Krawly ....

Cross currents converge of gratitude for being here, but
also greedy grasping – wanting more, wanting to be here
longer ... to be here, always with its clean creek and wide
sidewalks, America so green ...

So different from the town I'm from ... sinking into its
potholes ... e-coli in the water supply ... power cuts and
library budget gone ...

       "*Got everything ya need?*"

This heavenly ideal realm, clean organic ride,
so friendly – wholesome and good, even the beggars
are polite: "*How you doin', bro?*" Giving me the peace sign ...

while the next alienated white guy is ordering his weapons
online to take to the schoolyard firing line ... resentment
brewing into platoons preparing for the next invasion ... ...

while the four soldiers I meet seem so very nice, so stable,
so unashamed, so blasé about the wars they've fought and
are fighting still ... like Tongo taught: it's violence keeping
these sidewalks clean, lotta batons needed for Corso's
sweet prison dream ...

Still, reflecting on respect for connection, I regret not giving that beggar my organic tomato ... cause we're all together in this samsara ... both reaching for that top banana ...

"How you doin'? Got everything ya need?"

Fums boo wo ta za go pogiff –
Got everything ya need?
Rinzekeketo bee bee ...

Got everything you need?
Got something to believe?

Fums bo wo ta zee pogiff ... pogiff ...
dear me ... pogiff ... ...
Got everything ... got everything ...
got everything ...

The Wooden Veranda
(for Juanita)

    1.

Walking home from work
I passed the churches on Church Street,
Passed the donkeys on High.

I passed a lovely old home with a wooden veranda,
there next to the NG Kerk Saal, where
you can give your blood on a Tuesday.

I saw Juanita and Leonard
handing over the keys to the door
of the house with the wooden veranda.

And Leonard put his head on my shoulder,
and he said he was sad …

    2.

Thirty years isn't long,
if you're a Baobab.
If you're Yellow Wood,
Oak, or a Cycad,
thirty years isn't long.

Thirty years is pretty long
if you're a cat.
It's long to be in undergrad,
forever when you're young ...

    3.

We know a person from the language they use.
We know a person from the words they choose.
Because the world keeps speaking back to us,
and we see our texts reflected, coming back at us.

Listen to the words Juanita says:
She says "grounded",
she talks about "embodiment".
She might mention "integrity,"
she might call you "Flossie".
She says: "Ah, this bureaucracy,
 ... I should have left five years ago."

    4.

Surreal woman, soft and strong.
Ophelia hair, Egyptian eye-curl.
witchy tendrils spreading ...

5.

We like to think one day everything will be said,
everything will be heard, all the reasons why, justified.
Everything will be explained, right?

And we'll understand and we'll be understood.
And we'll say all the things we needed to say.
Surely, surely – surely one day there'll be time
to say everything to everyone ... all of it ... one day ...

And yet ... day by day,
there's just this falling away ...
this drifting slow-fade ... slipping,
disappearing and forgetting ...

Walking each other home, we're
passing on the keys to doors
of houses where our friends
don't live anymore.

Heimwee
(for my late grandmother)

Still feeling fresh off the boat,
anchored far from home ...

The cost of colonies
plays out in rage
at worlds destroyed
and remade,
by guns turning
texts into graves ...

Our sad state ...
too late to assimilate
Our unhappy heads.
Hoping we could blame it on
a choice we never
would have made,
between unequal dead ...

Futile longing to be home again
to be made whole again;
failed to make Europe here again,
and Europe doesn't want us back.

One Settler, One Pothole

Everyone is leaving town,
House prices are tumbling down.
Shops are closing, water off,
What are we chumps still doing around?

Seriously, though, can we drop the settler obsession?
I know it wasn't you, but before flaunting the word,
don't rub Elizabeth Salt into the wound, dude.
Don't stick it with pride on your signs: "Settler City".
Not everyone feels the same about a name. And it's a pity,
those who want to remain could reflect a little shame ...
even learn a word or two of those living here before you:
funda ukuthetha ulwimi lwabantu ...

If we hadn't robbed the car washers of their coin,
they might not have turned so mean, you know?
Let them earn a little income, bra.
If we'd chiselled our hearts open
tried to see it from the middle,
we'd have softened just a little.

These streets are cemented by centuries of rage.
Did the skirmishing ever end, or just shift off the page?

Ragtag refugees from all around –
impoverished Scottish, Fingo fleeing Mfecane ...
Despots and wars pretty normal in these parts.

I marvel at my friends in Zim still weathering the hungers there,
still cultivating inner worlds as dreams crumble around them.
I admire Alex's cob house on the edge of town,
a home made to fit her family, equipped with kindness.

So while everyone else is leaving town,
get your water tanks up and hunker down.
Time to put in clay floors instead of lawns.
If you don't fight the flow, you might not go under.

Everyone is leaving town, but
where does it end with the fleeing?
Sea levels are rising, ice caps amelt,
Vesuvius only sleeping ...

New Zealand juts unstable out on grumbling plates,
Europe's old, cold, its glories fading fast.
America's doomed, nukes pollute the earth,
and everybody's cousin has already moved to Perth.

Of course, we know not everything will be fine.
We're all for sure going to grow old, and sick, and die ...

But has the ship of the Monument sailed yet,
or is it still moored to the rock it's on?

Surely, not yet the last chopper outta Saigon ...

Afraid of Birds

On my walk to work, I love
to hear simple scales played clean
as I round the corner to the chapel
between green expanses of lawn
under monkey-puzzle trees.

I see the messy egrets have
found themselves a new abode.
I hope those below can stand
the clatter, accept their chatter,
stop chopping down their home.

The pigeon at Jane's Bistro
builds a nest of sodden cardboard,
gets upset by its reflection,
puffs its chest out, mesmerised.
Tries to scare itself away. Succeeds.

Moving House

Can hardly move,
without leaving a
line of words
trailing behind ...

More excretions
from this selfmind
      this imposter –
caught in the eddies
of memories no longer
entitled to,
      so slow
to let go
of these barnacles
slugging my base ...

      This rust grows
      quick.

Still here
      again,
still
      never again ...

Still here again.

Still
      gone.

Between One & Two Metres

(After watching Koleksiyoncu [The Collector, 2002], a Turkish film in which Pelin Esmer documents her uncle's obsession with collecting ...)

Everything Esmer's uncle buys,
he always buys one more:
one item to use, the other to store.

He buys two of every newspaper:
one from which to clip things out,
the other to preserve in plastic.

Neat piles
are stacked
in columns.

And he's observed that be-
tween one & two metres,
each tower topples over.

Esmer's uncle struggles to move around
a home that now features
corridors confined by mounds
stacked between one and two metres.

And he wishes he had two houses: one for his collections,
the other just to be in, to drink his tea in.

My mind is like this also,
eager to stack and store
every thought it thinks.

And I wish I had two minds:
one for the information,
the other just to breathe in.

Poor Seraphine

(After watching Seraphine [2008] by Martin Provost, about the Brut Art painter Séraphine Louis ...)

This washerwoman felt the cosmos in her,
even as she scraped floors, dried clothes,
wiped shit from chamber pots to pay the dye
to mix with butcher's blood and stolen wax
from holiest of holies, to shape the colours
she painted into being ...

Her marvellous mind released flowers with eyes,
leaves and trees exploding into suns,
her heart's flaming lips wet the night ...

... a small flare of kindness
from a person whom she trusted,
and Seraphine took wing, went wild ...

What bliss to be seen, to have been found!
Before, she'd quietly defied society,
and her daily humiliations rendered gold;
but when the world's flattery inflated her
she revelled in the acclaim,
craved a wedding dress, a castle –
came unbound ...

Poor Seraphine,
from hovel to spire
and back again ...

Poor Seraphine, again unseen,
reduced once more to solitary ecstasies,
glory illuminating her being ...

Poor Seraphine ...?
 ... poor us, locked out
of that mansion ...

Nichts Neueus

(After watching Im Westerns Nichts Neueus [All Quiet on the Western Front, 2022] and thinking of Ukraine ...)

A hundred years before this war,
which is already seeding
vengeance for the next,
Koestler in Kharkiv writes
the only stocks in store
were boot polish and condoms.

The Kommissars called the famine "a difficulty,"
while villages emptied and cannibals
lassoed prey in the streets for meat.

Fear and hatred: one breath apart.
Both fencing in the heart,
both searching spaces to be hid:
basement, bunker, tank.

How stop these vengeful spirits rising, solidifying?
How release identifying with this passing place?
How come back to body's breath while grieving?

Herder

(After watching Won't You Be My Neighbour? 2018 and A Beautiful Day in the Neighbourhood, 2019 both about Fred Rogers ...)

At the end of his life, Fred Rogers asks his wife:
"Was I sheep?"

And perhaps you'd think, who'd want to be sheeple?
Who'd want to be herd?

But she laughs, understands, it's so sweet, so absurd.
"Of course, you're a sheep."

"You've done everything right, you've been a
faithful follower of the Word."

Of course, he was also eccentric presenter,
his silly seriousness susceptible to scorn,
his kindness worn away at by a world of bleating billies.

Channelled

Fragments of the world blow through me.
I want to surrender, to let it happen ...

I want to stop hating, stop adversity.
I mean, my own. My aversion to others ...

The biggest project has always been the mind.
Art furthers spirit, animates material in decay.
Is the task of living interference, or submission?

Wild nature craves touch,
discovery of sense and place.
But who or what could own me,
least of all my self?

I keep slipping out of my own grasp.
Why ever do what we don't want to?
There's safety in release.
It's all a bout of consequences,
there are some that I don't care for.

Our vibration tunes to resonance.
Forest remains inside wild mind.
Is the tamed heart free?

Longing for a Rut

All my life been
longing for a rut.

Who are those strange souls
who find themselves routine?

Regularity, order, harmony
seem impossible dreams ...

River needs its riverbanks to
funnel its wilding stream.

Kinds of Wild

Dirt

Dirt between your toes,
let your hair grow.
Don't bother to brush.

Seed

Green cracks concrete,
persistent seed diverts.
Makes place for roots.

Warmth

Succulent on windowsill
recognizes warmth,
reaches for sun.

Tree

Inner spirit,
outside framed.
Hide inside your wild.

Forest

Aching to escape,
community's conclave.
Long for wider world outside.

Time

Domesticate your time.
Nail it down to programmed
pattern – canopied.

Space

Give way, create space,
stretch out horizon's line.
Is the sea wild, is the sky?

Wilderness

Let the punk poets enter the Care Ward,
meet the anguish of the aged.

The hard-nosed kids, the renegades,
those reaching for the edge and pushing,
those bright eyed for the abject –
let them meet the elderly.

Between the tidy beds in the garden of reason,
seeds fray into weeds sprouting delusion.

Sense windows kicked in, dull light, grey fog,
urine stains on sticky floors.

"Can you put the TV on?"
Dim and growing dimmer,
and for some – the fear.

Take warning, whirling bacchii cry:
"Fire destroys what it warms."

10 Characters

Nurse Marie

Her lapel is faded, and there's a lipstick smudge in the corner of her mouth. "It's an easy job," she says, as her needle sucks up an ampule. "You get to meet all sorts ..."

She likes doctors who don't wear shoes and laughs when she remembers one calling another a clown.
"He said: That clown?" and she laughs again.

She's curious about alternative medicine, but when the homeopath said she must crush the pumpkin pips on the full moon, she never went back.

Betty at the Beauty Parlour

The heavy woman's ready for her pedicure.
She's pleased to be spoiling herself. Says to the masseuse: "Sorry, I didn't cut my toenails, I knew I'd be coming here."
She's feeling luxurious, sure, but also sheepish ...

Anxious Annie

She remembers the walls of the Geesteswetenskappe Gebou. Roughly textured, they weren't quite smooth. Nervous about her exam, she scratched her knuckles up and down. Didn't notice the blood 'til it stained the paint.

Her Status

It made her sad when, with each passing year, she had to scroll further and further down the list of dropdown menus to find her year of birth; and yet, her romantic imagination soared whenever she had to enter a location.

She longed to enter somewhere else: Togo ... Laos ... Antigua ...

Online

She fell in love with him over his posts.
His updates were so funny.
But when they met, she was disappointed.
He was more into hip-hop, she was more into Keats. Worst was when he yelled out "Like!" at every second thing she said.

The Administrator

Edwin enjoyed organising and ordering his world.
He could lose himself in the flow of lists, the naming of folders; loved arranging 'activities outstanding'.
The Excel was open, and Edwin was at peace.

Guy

The guy's tongue feels out a chip in his tooth.
"It's a part of my life," he sighs, "which I'll never get back."
She also sighs.
"I'm always going to have this gap, can you see it ...?"
She: "No."
He: "But I'll always know what's not there."
She sighs again.

Tannie

She arches a purple eyebrow:
"*Nee wat, as dit is hoe die Boeddhiste Kersfees vier
dan weet ek nie meer mooi nie ...*"

Electrician

Dude in bulging overalls and accent blusters in
to fix the blinds.
The academics stand by, coy; their ironic patter having
failed entirely to shield them from the sun.

Imaginary Theatres: A Bad Spell

Past

You're on a slow road out of the Karoo. It's hot and dry and all of your ex-girlfriends are hitching out of Cradock. They're standing there where they sell the mini metal windmills near the turn off to the memorial for the Cradock Four, which you really should make time for but you've driven too far past by now.

You don't have enough room for all of your exes, so you stop at the furthest point, closest to your first ex-girlfriend to enable a quick getaway before the others can catch up. And as your four fastest ex-girlfriends pile into the car, the wire windmill sellers form a chorus and sing extracts from *Boesman and Lena* while doing a pantsula routine before marching up Karoo's Tafelberg.

You drive away, picking up speed between the weirdly shaped outcrops. On top of each peak, barely visible, are replicas of ex-girlfriends dressed as Olive Schreiner doing voice exercises, while men wearing volksklere play jukskei in the square before nagmaal.

A low flying aeroplane appears pulling a streaming banner screaming: "Apathy Now!", but it's accidentally shot out of the sky by a nuclear submarine without a captain. He'd been delayed because the buses ordered by the Cape City Council had doors installed on the wrong side, so when he'd tried to disembark, the captain stepped into traffic.

Present

Taps are turned and precious water is wasted in exuberant displays of outrage flooding computer labs and lecture venues. The flood douses cars still burning from a former fire. A joyful fury takes hold.

Police join the dance, rhythmically bouncing rubber bullets off shoulders, off elbows, off knees. The dance becomes ever more frenetic, singing "Put that bottle down, put it down". The State is the wallflower at the party. It takes a while to join in. It's waiting for a different tune, something that won't draw too much attention to itself. It's shy, self-conscious.

Inmates set fire to their prison and find themselves trapped in smoke. "Free at last", they lament, as their cells choke them into darkness.

Somewhere else a roomful of people are sweating as they spin the wheels of mounted bicycles going nowhere to ambient rhythms.

Future

Protest becomes institutionalised. Classes teach its history; researchers explore framing mechanisms. Students attend workshops where they learn how to dislocate systems, how to disrupt better. The workshops break down when the students protest the classes.

"Yes," the teacher encourages,
"Excellent! Now you're getting it."

The students carve an A+ into the teacher's chest with a Bic ballpoint pen, opening his veins to jot notes in their little red books.

You chase the horizon. The horizon does what it does.

the programmable bride

the man gently opens up the machine and finding an agreeable port for his firm flash, he eagerly installs his software ...

once booted up, the man takes his first tentative steps, finding his bride perfect in every way, already completely in love, and dreamy ...

the man tenderly reaches out for her – she understands him so well, she's concerned about his needs, she wants to know how he feels, wants only to please, she only –

/ but – there's an interruption /

somebody's on the stairs, someone's knocking at his door – the man is forced to close her down a little too abruptly ...

while he's away he can't wait to get back, he thinks about her all the time, longs to flip his laptop lid up, to open her ...

but when he finally and silently prises open the instrument of his heart's desires, she seems disorientated ...

he didn't shut her down properly, never filed the folders into their allotted compartments, she takes a little longer to load ...

she's still utterly charming, sure, completely present, and yet he detects an edge to the calibrations of her voice modulator ...

nevertheless, they soon engage in ways immeasurably meaningful and again the warmth is back: there's charm & artlessness in her smile, sincerity in each reply ... till there's –

/ again – an interruption /

their interaction's cut short because the cat has pissed on the plug and the whole thing has gone up in an electric mess of wires burnt black ... the man had better fix the fuses and wash the mat and bury the cat ...

now, every time the flow between the man and his flawless creation has been interrupted, she's been getting a little more insecure, a little more uncertain ...

he's doing his best here:
he backs her up,
he defrags her disks;
but the guy is only human,
and sometimes his attention slips ...

and sometimes tiny flakes of skin
settle into his keyboard,
finding their way into her processors ...

after his fifth or sixth attempt
to shut the system down safely and securely,
after the plug's been pulled one time too many,
the man notices that her trust is wearing thin and ...

she's becoming impatient, finding fault, her smile less
convincing, she's taking longer to load, slower to warm up ...
when did she get so serious?

the man doesn't know what to do,
he's getting frustrated
even when she does appear,
she seems so pixelated ...
/ ... until ... /

she can't remember who he is,
perhaps she's been hacked,
has she slipped a disc,
attracted a virus ...?

whatever the case may be,
eventually, the programmable bride
will not boot up at all ...

not even in safe mode,
not even in the sandbox.

is it really too late ...
isn't there an update?

ten thousand hands

ten thousand hands remove the stage, come close and clap ... they want to speak – the hands want to say where they've been, what they've touched; but they're silent, dumb, blind ... the hands have no words ...

the hands have nowhere else to be ... the hands wait for orders: when to stiffen, to curl; how to hold, to touch, to point, salute; the hands keep coming back, they breed, they get further and closer, the hands want to help, they want to explain, they want to hide behind other hands ... the hands want to plan, they want to chart, to jot, to outline ... they curl into a fist ...

the hands have places to be, they want gloves to help them tighten snug against the cold, the hands want to go to tahiti to meet a margaret mead girl on the beach; they want to reach over and lotion her bronzed back ... the hands want to attack anyone who harms her, they want to soldier on ...

the hands want to meet other hands, to protect, to craft, create... the hands want to reach out, they want to reach back, to dig, to search inside, they want to feel how tight it is, how smooth; the hands want to turn back time, they want to begin again, trim the nails, push back the beds, to rest ... the hands want to befriend other hands: soften, palm to palm
  ... fingers crossed ...

so i had this really

so i had this really strange dream where i was walking around naked, but unlike other walking-around-naked dreams, in this one i was feeling kinda bolshy, yea, just strolling around sort of all, well, cocky, and pleased ...

and i was about to go into this lecture to talk to a roomful of people, and i realised my appearance was gonna be kinda funny and surprising, but i was almost looking forward to it – just walking in there large as life and pleased as might be, naked, into this roomful of people ...

but then, just before i got to the door i noticed that my penis was looking kinda shrivelly and i thought, ah, dang, man what now? and so i duck into this side room, laundry room kinda place next door to the door to the roomful of people, and i find this plastic 2 litre ice-cream tub on a shelf and i fill it with warm water and put my penis in there ...

and then a really strange thing happens: as soon as my penis was in the tub, it sorta starts lapping up the water as though it's real thirsty, and pretty soon it's looking fat and sleek like a lil' slug just soaking away and enjoying itself in there, and i'm looking down at it kind of friendly and proprietorial-like, and I wake up, going, aw, man, it's just like a little lamb ...

clint's koan

so, i was in settlers hospital. getting my, you know, the old snip. what's it called? not quite castration, but almost. okay, yes, vasectomy, i was getting a vasectomy at settler's hospital. what can, what can one even say about that ...? the reasons why, the offer of manhood on the altar of marriage, accepting once and for all there would be no hereafters ...

so i was lying there, deed done, watching that little mounted television high up in the corner, and there was clint eastwood being interviewed by this beautiful reporter who was clearly very much enamoured of him. and clint was real sincere, he'd just, like, flown his helicopter to the set he was directing, and she was catching him during a coffee break, asking all the usual questions about his 'secrets of success,' and such ...

and his answer was real clear, uncomplicated. he said he's just trying to do his best in whatever situation he's in, clint said – we're having this interview, right? and i'm giving you my attention and i'm listening to you, and i'm answering your questions ... and i thought, cool, thanks, nice, great lesson ... so there it is: the message from eastwood – clint's koan.

at the funeral

he'd spoken to me the week before, asked an extension on his assignment, told me his girlfriend had just suicided ... it was an awkward scene, right, because there was a meeting coming up and the room started filling with staff and we were caught off guard ... i said of course, no problem, so sorry, extension granted, sure, but I didn't follow up on his distress ... and then the next week he was gone ...

at the funeral, his parents tried to cover up their horror in a 'celebration of his life' ... his friends were dressed brightly and an ex sang a cheerful song ... his red-eyed father was holding on to his ill-fitting half moustache to keep his side of their bargain to do 'mo-vember' together ...

i wished for the nerve to step up to that mic and prick the boil of that repression, to speak true and clear and make that church weep the sorrow it was longing to show ... they were afraid, of course ... and i was also afraid ... i was scared to dent the veneer they were trying so hard to maintain ...

why shake us into the truth of what we could have done?... why remind us of how desperately we need each other ... even now, every day ... ... even as we jog along, dry eyes blind ...

garbage

travelling india and africa
one gets inured to garbage –
tho it almost seems more natural
not to hide it, right?

why pretend it's disappeared?

today my eyes widened at
europe's clean streets:
that metal sign slammed into earth,
asphalt shaping the road and
plastic painted over everything.

those buildings, these cars –
there's debris everywhere ...

notifications

you want to reach out, but
your world is silent, since you
disabled your notifications.

you want to tell her everything
that's wrong with you, with her;
but you disabled your notifications.

feather dancing in the cold air falling,
planet breathing, night sky quiet,
since you disabled your notifications.

in two hours, i will have been awake for twenty-four ...

if i'm still awake, that is ....

have a mouth guard in,
read a book on berlin

i ... i ... i ... i ... i ...

had a meeting with a student,
& we read a gertrude stein play
to see what it was like
and if it took her interest
in landscape any further ....
      like ... like ...
         all about landscape

  and the repetition
  and the landscape
  and the repetition ...

hosted my comedy improv students' show,
chaired a management meeting,
had a nap on my back, then a lot of caffeine,
also tincture, glass of wine, too many sandwiches...
almost feel like one now, with melted cheese ... hmm ...

walked with louise in the gardens
when she brought me lunch:
2 boiled eggs and a sandwich.

    can't avoid the repetition
    and the landscape
    and the repetition ...

in one hour and fifty-five
i will have been awake
for twenty-four.

if i'm still awake, that is ...

next door's addict begs her fix,
it's the dealer's "baby mama".
"tupac," she calls out, "papa" ...

lou is fearless, confronts them.
i don't get involved, even after
stones thrown by baby mama,
clatter our rooftop –
she's out of her mind with need.

am i still awake, that is ...

questionnaire

do you remember those wire coat hangers that
you'd unwind to help you sidle up the doorknob
if your keys were stuck inside your car?

do you also hold your breath when you see a character
underwater on the screen, wonder if you can outlast them?

do you enjoy the sound a spade makes
when it liberates the earth?
do you hope your life will get better,
though suspect it may get worse?

do you feel not necessarily hard done by,
but done by, nonetheless …?
or do you feel grateful for getting
what you didn't deserve and then
guilty for being so very lucky?

do you long for someone to talk to,
someone who creates speech in you,
who feeds your speaking with their listening?

do you ever feel astonished to be alive at all?

do you see your future – hazy, vague, dissolving …
your real future, I mean … 1000 years …

everybody is a bridge

everybody is a bridge
the web weaves the folds
holding us to this grid.

we're connected to each other
every brother has a mother,
every other an another.

web of diamonds weaves the world
each reflection's a protection.
everybody's a connection.

everybody is a bridge
the web weaves the fold
holding us to this grid.

we see what shines through,
and your answer's what you ask
every mirror is a mask.

everybody is a bridge
is it me, or is it you – ?
are you reflection or projection
or the light that's shining through?

revolutionary diaries (tryp on anxious conflicts)

1   this well-meaning ire's gonna land us in the fire ...

i want to speak out, but i'm afraid ...
afraid of the good people, the well-meaning ...
afraid of those itching for a fight,
afraid of the marchers and their causes ...

there's violence in the flower
forced into the gun barrel
violence in the cynical smirk ...

2   mob

fear returns,
chanting in the streets.

who's the real enemy
– sickness or old age –
what's to rail against?

rage against disease,
anger at growing old ...

3   on dealing with monsters

avoid them, engage them,
stay away from their claws.
become them, embrace them,
forgive all their wars ...

you see the devil everywhere

in the appearance of cats, rats, moles
in the couch surfers from slovenia
in the mess of shoes on the floor

you see the devil everywhere

keep the devil at bay
keep the door seal framed
keep the windows crossed

when everything's on fire
you're deaf to the mewling
of the kitten on the kitchen ledge

hope

flower fights the wall,
sparrow pecks at dirt.

there's a phantom seat inside of me,
bones remember birth.

lou hopes the plumber comes,
and the man to check the gutters.

i hope the candle lasts the night,
an unwritten manuscript mutters.

on turning 40

… will i regret not
having adventured more,
met more people and places?
or, will I be glad to have stayed
sometimes sober …?

reasonably well travelled,
fattening and bald,
dotted all the i's, but
not enough awards …

the writer

I

there was a man obsessed with writing down the past ...
it began as diary, recording events of the day, but soon took
over his whole existence until he couldn't drink a cup of tea
without recording what he thought of it – (hmm ... needs
honey, hmm ...) – he couldn't have a conversation without
transcribing it ... everything that occurred had to be put down
into words, words, words ...

II

one day the man found himself fascinated by the future ...
he began to make lists, write down plans ... the man wrote
schedules for the week ahead: sunrise, sunset, shows to
watch, things to do ... everything was scratched down in his
books ...

III

and then one day the man disappeared ... gone ... nobody
missed him but then the neighbour's dog began barking at the
stench ... and when they broke the doors down they found his
body withered at his desk, a thousand pages filled with:

"i am writing ... i am writing ... i am writing ..."

Anton's great great great grandfather, painter unknown

Robyn Oosthysen

Anton Krueger's poems have appeared in *New Coin, Itch, Aerial, Botsotso, Ons Klyntij, Litnet, Green Dragon, Big Bridge, African Writing, Incwadi, Alookaway, Laugh it Off, Tyhini, Sweet Magazine, Mahala, Kotaz, Aerodrome, Kagablog, Business Day, The Pretoria News, Sicak Nal* **(in Turkish); and** *Consciousness, Literature and the Arts.*

He was the first English poetry editor for Litnet and from 1997-2001, was part of the "Bekgeveg" team performing monthly at venues all over Pretoria and Johannesburg, as well as at the Klein Karoo Kunstefees and Aardklop festivals. Poems from this era were published in the anthology *Six of the Best* (1998, Poets Press). He was invited to perform at Poetry Africa in 2008 and in 2023. His first anthology, *Everyday Anomalies* appeared in 2011 (Aerial) and in the same year his poem "Nine Notes on Lisbon" was a runner up for the Dalro poetry prize.

Over the last few years, Anton has been experimenting with improvised spoken word collaborations with a variety of musicians and DJ's, including Tony Bentel and Francois le Roux (the HA! man). Anton has also published plays, memoir, short stories, criticism and arts journalism. He lives in Makhanda where he heads the Department of Literary Studies in English at Rhodes University.

Still, Anton considers himself an amateurist, inspired by love rather than profit, gift instead of commodity. To sample his work, visit:

https://amateurist.weebly.com/writings.html

Selections from *Everybody is a Bridge* have been performed in collaboration with improvisations on piano by Paul Hanmer.